SUMMARY

The aim of this field guide is to prepare you for what might happen when in a hostile environment, and how to avoid bad situations as best as you can.

It also guides you to what to do if you end up in trouble and being caught in a situation you did not plan on.

The key is 'situational awareness'.

HEAT training, by trained individuals, is highly recommended prior to travel to a hostile environment and this field guide serves as a reminder on what you will be taught.

Do not assume that bad things only happen to other people. Avoid, prepare and be prepared.

STAY ALERT

STAY AWARE

STAY SAFE

Contents

White	Unprepared and unready to take action.
Yellow	Prepared, alert & relaxed. Good situational awareness.
Orange	Alert to probable danger. Ready to take action.
Red	Action Mode. Focused on the emergency at hand.
Black	Panic. Breakdown of physical & mental performance.

Being situationally aware will often save you by not placing you in a dangerous way in the first place – BY AVOIDING the problem.

Situational Awareness is being aware of your surroundings – knowing what's going on around you – and identifying potential threats, criminal behavior, and dangerous situations.

"Situational awareness is more of a mindset than a skill". It can be practiced by anyone and could be a life saver.

One should always be in the YELLOW state above at a minimum and ideally in the ORANGE, especially when travelling to a dangerous area.

In every dangerous instance the best way to stay safe is to AVOID the problem in the first place. Being situationally aware will be instrumental in helping you AVOID problems; and if you do get caught up in an incident, it will help you react and evacuate safely.

Here are four steps to improve your situational awareness:

Recognize That Threats Exist

Accept that threats exist – and they may exist within your proximity during your day-to-day travels. Many people have a normalcy bias and have little consideration for their own security while living in perceived safety. A false sense of security can be deadly.

Take Responsibility for Your Own Security

The police are not everywhere, and YOU are the first line of responsibility. You need to look out for yourself, and not succumb to a mindset that someone else will protect you.

Trust Your Gut or Intuition

You know that 'voice' of intuition in the back of your head? You probably should not ignore it. Apparently, many victims who experienced feelings of danger prior to an incident – chose to ignore them (and therefore became victims). Your semi-subconscious mind, coupled with your senses, have ways of alerting you to potential danger – if only you 'listen' to it.

Conscious Effort to Practice Situational Awareness

The final step is to do it. Discipline yourself to consciously practice situational awareness. Pay attention to what's happening around you, your gut feelings, and to stay 'in the YELLOW' (relaxed alert). Practice being alert to your surroundings, even while you're distracted or busy. Actively use your eyes and ears and scrutinize what they pick up – make it a habit.

Here are a few drills that you can do to improve your situational awareness skills.

1. Identify all the exits when you enter a building.

2. Count the number of people in a restaurant, subway or train car.

3. Note which cars take the same turns in traffic.

4. Look at the people around you and attempt to figure out their stories. Imagine what they do for a living, their mood, what they are focused on and what it appears they are preparing to do, based merely on observation.

5. Next time you're in a parking lot, look for – and count – the number of cars with people sitting in them, whether you're walking to the storefront, or coming back to your car, or even driving through.

Engaging in such simple situational-awareness drills will train a person's mind to be aware of these things almost subconsciously when the person is in a relaxed state of awareness.

STAY ALERT

STAY AWARE

STAY SAFE

SECURITY AT HOME.

A crime against you is most likely going to occur near or in your home. Here are suggestions to help prevent crime or in the event of a home invasion:

- Pre-warn your security staff of your arrival so they can open and close the gate quickly on your arrival. Check the gate is free of people before entering.

- Make sure that you have an alarm response company and that your staff have access to a button.

- Train your employees / family so that no one enters the premises without your permission or only with a company and personal ID (electricity, water companies).

- Ensure your windows and doors have grills.

- Lock your external grills when you are in the house but not in bed – day or night.

- If you have dogs, some should stay in the house at night.

- Ensure the people you live with (partner and children) know what to do and where to go in the event of an attempted break-in.

- Always keep a phone in the bedroom (with speed dial numbers) so you can call out in the event of an emergency.

- Have a safe room that everyone in the house moves to while locking doors behind you on the way to the safe room.

- Make sure that you can make calls (signal) from the safe room.

FAILURE TO PREPARE IS PREPARING TO FAIL

Keep in mind that you need to get to your destination smoothly, safely and with the minimum of fuss and bother. These tips will help you achieve this.

- Do not draw attention to yourself and do not become the focus of attention – BE THE GREY PERSON.
- Dress in comfortable, dull, hard-wearing clothes - do not wear 'patriotic' or military type clothing or anything too loud.
- Wear strong, closed shoes – not sandals or flip flops. Best if they are easy to remove and put on for security gates and emergencies – not with a lot of laces
- Reduce jewelry to a bare minimum.
- Understand the climate well and pack accordingly – sunblock, hat, sunglasses etc.

- Understand the time zone of the country you are in and that of
your home country and recognize and remember the difference.

FAILURE TO PREPARE IS PREPARING TO FAIL

Research the country you are visiting, online and on the news.

- Gather as much information from colleagues and family.

- Prepare your family for what they might see on the news.

- Conduct a personal risk assessment of the areas you are visiting.

Research the following:

- Cultures and Customs (religion, dress codes etc.)

- Climate (what clothes to take). Natural hazards (tsunami, earthquake, etc.)

- Money / financial situation - Research carefully how you will access money if you need to. Best is to use ATMs if available, so carry cards and cash. Ensure your credit card company is aware of you travelling and to which country.

- Visa requirements.

- Medical requirements / vaccinations and Health issues (prevalence of malaria, yellow fever, Ebola etc.)

- Medical facilities in the country including dentists and vets (vets can be used in emergency situations if you need emergency care).

Research the following...cont.

- Current political situation (terrorism, riot risk etc.)

- Local knowledge of crime rates and areas encountered.

- Best hotels for safety and location.

- Best mode of travel in the country.

- Consulate information – location and contacts.

- Power requirements – plug types and voltage – 110 or 240 V.

Prepare the following well before departure:

- Update or create a will.
- Create a power of attorney.
- Ensure your family have access to funds in your absence.

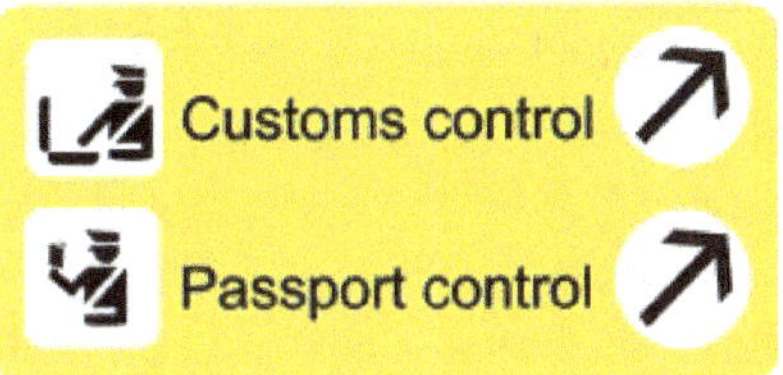

FAILURE TO PREPARE IS PREPARING TO FAIL

Prepare all the documents you will need in advance of travel:

- Ensure you have copies of all important documents in a separate and safe place either with your person or in your luggage.

- Make scans of all important documents and save them on a flash disk and carry them in a safe place with your person always.

- Ensure your work or families also have copies of all your important documents.

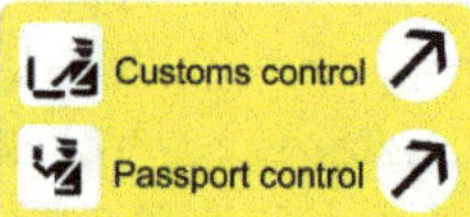

FAILURE TO PREPARE IS PREPARING TO FAIL

Documents and other important items you will need:

- Up to date passport.

- Visa and / or work permits – incl. letter from your employer / host.

- All your medical requirements – see page 6.

- Consulate locations and contacts.

- Insurance documents – life, medical and evacuation.

- Cash – carry different currencies particularly US$, Euro and Sterling.

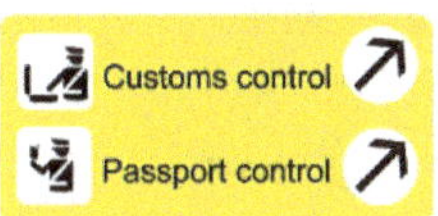

FAILURE TO PREPARE IS PREPARING TO FAIL

Documents and other important items you will need...cont.

- Credit and Debit cards – kept in a safe place.

- Airline tickets, reference numbers and itineraries.

- Next of kin contact list.

- Map of country and cities you are visiting.

- Driving license (ideally International) if you plan to drive.

ALL THE ABOVE MUST BE CARRIED WITH YOU ALWAYS.

COPIES MUST BE KEPT IN ANOTHER SECURE LOCATION.

LEAVE ANOTHER SET OF COPIES AT HOME.

FAILURE TO PREPARE IS PREPARING TO FAIL

Let all your family and colleagues know where you are going and for how long.

- Establish a communication plan with your family and colleagues.

- Know what communications are available – networks, roaming etc.

- Ensure your phones are on roaming (check charges) and you can top-up if on pre-pay plan.

- Ideally carry 2 phones that use different networks and ensure all contacts are on both phones.

- If you don't have roaming make sure that as a priority, you get a local SIM card and load it with plenty of credit.

FAILURE TO PREPARE IS PREPARING TO FAIL

- Always carry a charger cable, adaptor for the relevant sockets in the country and ideally a charged external battery pack.

- Have quick dial numbers programmed – to work, family, consulate, hotel etc.

- Also, have a printout of important / emergency numbers in a separate location.

FAILURE TO PREPARE IS PREPARING TO FAIL

Know who you will call in the event of an emergency:

- Office HQ.
- Hospitals, dentists, vets.
- Insurance providers.
- Police.
- Hotel reception.
- Consulate.
- Family.

FAILURE TO PREPARE IS PREPARING TO FAIL

ALSO:

- Carry all the relevant power chargers you need for your appliances – computer, phones etc.

- Carry a few cables for your phone and a cigarette lighter adapter.

- Carry spare batteries for the appliances you are carrying as they can be expensive or unavailable.

REGISTER WITH YOUR CONSULATE EITHER PRIOR TO DEPARTURE OR IMMEDIATELY UPON ARRIVAL.

GIVE THEM YOUR DETAILS AND TRAVEL PLANS FOR THE DURATION OF YOUR VISIT.

FAILURE TO PREPARE IS PREPARING TO FAIL

Make sure you are physically and mentally fit prior to departure and consider a medical examination prior to departure.

- Ensure you have accident and life insurance in place and know where insurance can and cannot be used in the country of travel.

- Ensure you have Medical Evacuation Insurance, let them know you are travelling and have the contact details on fast dial.

- Ensure all your vaccinations are up to date and carry all relevant vaccination certificates.

- Ensure that all inoculations are up to date, and you have the relevant inoculations for the country you are visiting.

FAILURE TO PREPARE IS PREPARING TO FAIL

- Make sure you carry enough of any prescribed medications you may need for the duration and carry the prescription with you.

- If you have any allergies, make sure that these can be identified quickly in the event of an emergency if you are not able to communicate. (bracelet, tattoo etc.)

- Make sure your blood group information is available.

FAILURE TO PREPARE IS PREPARING TO FAIL

When travelling try and carry the following depending on your length of stay, location and requirements while there:

- A main bag that ideally has a hard case to use as a lockable storage device when in the hotel. This can be as large or small as you require (some people like to travel light and not check bags in at airports).

- A small backpack that you can use as your day to day carry bag which could also be your 'Grab bag' – see below.

- A money pouch that you carry concealed around your waist that carries the bulk of your money and any important documents such as passports etc.

- You may also need a brief case for work, or utilize the 'Grab' backpack for carrying laptops etc.

FAILURE TO PREPARE IS PREPARING TO FAIL

<u>Grab Bag Contents</u>

Ideally you should have a small backpack that you grab in the event of an emergency, and you need to evacuate a situation or place quickly.

- Passport, ID and any other important identity documents.
- Copies of your travel documents (hard copy or flash disk)
- Cash in the foreign currency (ideally at least $500).
- A small First Aid kit WITH Sunscreen and useful drugs such as Paracetamol and a small supply of your prescription medication.
- Small water bottle and small amount of food (like nuts and raisins).
- Torch and / or a head torch with spare batteries.
- Light spare clothing including a warm fleece and hat (to suit location) and spare socks.
- Swiss army knife or Leatherman.

Grab Bag Contents...Cont.

- Lighter or matches.

- Toilet paper or tissues.

- Notebook and a couple of pens AND Map of location you are in.

- Phone charger, external battery pack or spare battery for phone.

You could also go as far as:

- Water purification tabs.
- Sewing kit and fishing kit with extra cord.
- Rain poncho or small tarp.
- Compass or GPS.

This list is endless so try and keep it light and compact.

DEPARTURE – Travel by Air & Aviation Security (AVSEC)

Remember - be the "grey" person – do not wear loud clothing or jewelry.

- Always be very aware of your surroundings as soon as you enter the airport. Also, always be aware of other passengers.

- Move as quickly as possible and process through check-in, security and immigration as quickly as you can. The most dangerous time at an airport is prior to security.

- Do not use corporate logos on your luggage.

- When checking in ask for a window seat near an exit – in the event of a hijack, the aisle seat passengers will be struck more often.

- When in the airport and on board avoid working on your computer while dealing with company or confidential information – keep in mind that other people can see you work, so use devices that only allow you to see the screen.

- If speaking on your phone, do so quietly. Other people can hear what you are saying.

Airports that you are not familiar with can be noisy, congested, confusing and hostile. You could be new in that environment; you could stand out and you will likely be in a position of weakness. These points may help you move quickly, safely and smoothly out of the airport:

- As soon as you enter the airport off the airplane, be very aware of your surroundings. Also, always be aware of other passengers.

- Make sure that you keep your family and colleagues informed of your progress and of any changes whenever you can in your travel plans.

- On arrival make sure you know who is collecting you. If it is a taxi or chauffer service, ask them not to use your name on the name board. Have an agreed pseudo name.

- Ideally if you do not know the person picking you up, send the driver a picture of yourself and have a picture of the driver so you both know each other prior to arrival.

- Move as quickly as you can through the secured area and baggage area to the lobby and into your transport and leave the airport as quickly as possible.

- Text or call the driver when you are about to exit the lobby area. Ensure you have the driver's contacts prior to arrival.

- Know where you are going to as you leave the airport, and ideally familiarize yourself with the route to your hotel / office and any familiar landmarks en-route.

HOTEL / ACCOMMODATION - Security & Awareness

When choosing a hotel always consider the following:

- Firstly, ask other people for suggestions of safe places they may have stayed in before.

- Ideally have your security provider or local office staff carry out a security survey before your arrival.

- Avoid hotels with no visible security from the outside of the hotel.

- Check that the only modes of entry are through official entry points – i.e.: evacuation doors are secure form the outside.

- In a multi-story hotel, book a room on the 3rd, 4th or 5th floors facing away from the main road. (thieves, fire, bomb blast).

At check-in

- At check-in always keep your bags and belongings in sight and near you – theft and tampering can occur in hotel lobbies.

- Ask the check-in staff or concierge about any available information about the area – where to avoid etc.

- As you walk to your room make yourself aware of the route you took, fire exits, fire extinguishers and imagine how you would exit in an emergency and where you would go.

- Make the porters aware that you are observant of your belongings and surroundings.

- Get a contact list of important hotel staff and all their numbers.

- Avoid using your home address when registering – use your office address.

- Do not let reception know of your appointments too far in advance – if at all.

- Identify areas you can get cover from view and / or cover from fire.

After check-in and during your stay

- Take a moment soon after check-in to make yourself familiar with the layout of the hotel – take a slow walk around the whole facility.

- Become familiar with the hotel evacuation procedures by reading the in-room information pack and behind the hotel door.

- Assume all calls are tracked and even go so far as assuming the room could be bugged. Be cautious of your conversations and email traffic while using hotel Wi-Fi.

- Carry a rubber door stop jam to use on the inside of your door while you are in the room or in the shower.

- Always Have your 'Grab' bag ready – see section on grab bag contents.

- Keep the deadbolt in place, lights on and the room locked when inside the room.

- Know who is calling you and for what reason – if you get a strange call ask them to transfer you to another extension (reception). If they hang up, you know it was not the hotel.

- Do not accept anything that you have not ordered into the room.

- Any visitors should be met in the lobby – not in your room. If someone comes to your door, use the peep hole and check with reception if need be if the hotel sent someone.

While out of your room

- Avoid leaving your key / card at hotel reception when you are out.

- Leave the TV on, lights on and the 'Do Not Disturb' sign on the door.

- Do not use 'clean room' signs as this indicates your absence. Try and get housekeeping to clean the room while you are there or at breakfast.

- Ensure you use the hotel safes in the room – do not use the reception safe.

- While out of the room lock your computer, large valuables and any important documents in a lockable hard suitcase.

Always be aware of your surroundings and other cars / people around you / following you – even if the driver is not.

- The use of mirrors is imperative – often.

- Ideally travel with more than one person in your car (not incl. the driver).

- If walking, always travel with another person or a group.

- Keep your important belongings always close to you or hidden on your body.

- Don't isolate yourself. Ensure you stay in populated well-lit areas. Do not enter unsafe areas unless necessary.

- Avoid walking and driving at night where possible.

- Avoid areas frequented by Westerners and / or foreign named places (McDonalds).

- Always keep a copy of all your important documents with you.

- Travel with a phone charger (with cigarette lighter adapter) in case you end up being away from your hotel/office longer than expected and / or stuck in traffic for long periods.

Do not self-drive in a foreign country unless necessary.

- Always wear seatbelts.

- Keep windows up and doors locked.

- Do not open windows or doors to strangers.

- Always remain in the car unless it is dangerous to do so.

- Make sure your driver follows rules of the road and speed limits and drives in a safe manner.

- Don't be a good Samaritan unless it is a person you know.

- Don't allow the driver to let unauthorized passengers in the car without you knowing the other person.

- Use only licensed companies if using a taxi. And agree on a fare prior to entering a taxi.

- If driving yourself:
    - Drive at the fastest safe speed.
    - Keep in the outside lane in heavy traffic in case you need to drive off the road.
    - Always maintain at least one vehicle length separation to allow maneuver and/or escape if necessary.
    - Always be aware of all traffic situations and look ahead for possible issues.

KEEP YOUR FRIENDS AND COLLEAGUES AWARE OF YOUR MOVEMENTS AT ALL TIMES WHEN TRANSITING (BY BOTH ROAD AND AIR) AND ADVISE THEM ONCE YOU HAVE ARRIVED SAFELY AT EACH DESTINATION.

If driving yourself or being driven, make sure that you can rely on the vehicle; it is your lifeline. Do not accept being driven in a vehicle that may fail.

Check the following on your vehicle:

- Engine oil.
- Engine coolant.
- Fuel.
- Tires – pressures and tread.
- Spare tire – present and correct size and not flat.
- Jack and jack handle.
- Wheel spanner.
- Small tool kit.

ON THE MOVE – Vehicle Check Point (VCP)

VCPs could be illegal or legal and you may not be able to tell the difference at the time. Be prepared for either, as follows:

- Ensure all the passengers know where the rendezvous point is should you have to exit and run away from the car – for example 500 mtrs back on the road you have just come on.

- Reduce speed and do as directed – pull over, stop, continue....

- Dip lights if at night and consider putting on the internal light.

- Make sure all in the vehicle remain calm, with hands visible and no rapid movements.

- Ask a passenger to get on the phone (or do so yourself when possible) and inform colleagues of the location and situation.

In the event of checkpoint...cont.

- Keep your doors locked and windows up except the driver who should only put the window down enough to talk to whoever has stopped them.

- Make sure the driver is aware of an escape route and keep this clear and the vehicle in gear.

- Be polite and friendly and have documents ready – IDs, driving licenses etc.

- Show any documents required but try not to surrender them.

- All to always stay in the car unless otherwise directed.

In the event of checkpoint...cont.

- The driver must always try and keep control of the car keys – consider having a spare key in an easy to access location (under dash or taped to roof rack.)

- Observe any searches and protest if the searcher tries to remove items from the vehicle.

- Carry small denominations of cash at hand and tradable items such as cigarettes.

- If things go wrong try and stay with the car, otherwise escape on foot and go to the rendezvous point.

IN THE EVENT YOU ARE DRIVING, THE BELOW ARE THE RECOMMENDED STEPS IN THE EVENT OF AN RTA.

IF YOU FEEL YOUR LIFE IS AT RISK DUE TO A MOB, THEN DRIVE TO THE NEAREST POLICE STATION AND TELL THEM WHAT HAS HAPPENED AND WHY YOU LEFT THE SCENE.

Stop.

If you are involved in an accident that causes injury to or the death of anyone, or which causes damage to property or any animal, you are required by law to stop your vehicle.

It is a crime not to stop after an accident in most countries. If your life is under immediate threat if you stay at the accident, drive straight to the nearest police station and explain why you left and return with them to the scene if required.

Help anyone who is hurt.

After you have stopped, you need to find out if anyone is hurt and help them as much as you can. You also need to call emergency services.

If you don't know anything about first aid, be careful not to do anything that might make the injury worse.

Unless you yourself need to go for help, you must stay at the scene until a police officer says you can leave.

Find out what the extent of the damage is.

You will need to find out how much damage has been caused to the property. You need to give your name and address and vehicle registration number to the other party / police.

Get all relevant information.

If you are involved in the accident, you should try to get the following information from all parties involved and witnesses:

- Full names.

- ID numbers.

- Addresses.

- Telephone numbers.

- Vehicle registration numbers.

- Descriptions of the vehicles.

- Details of police and traffic officers and ambulance personnel.

- Details of tow truck personnel.

This information will help you if you want to make a claim against your insurance or if you want to claim the costs of repairs from the other party.

At a later stage, you or your lawyers may need a copy of the accident report that is filled out by the police.

Report the accident to the police.

Wait for the Police to arrive OR if you can, call them and tell them where you are and what has happened.

Do not interfere with the evidence.

If anyone is injured in an accident, the vehicles may not be moved before the police or traffic officer has arrived and said that the vehicles can be moved.

If the accident totally blocks the passage of other vehicles, the vehicle may be moved sufficiently to allow vehicles to pass, but only after you have clearly marked the vehicle positions (for example with chalk or spray paint).

Be aware of the legal consequences.

Some of the possible legal consequences following an accident are:

- A criminal charge of driving recklessly.
- A criminal charge of driving negligently.
- A criminal charge of culpable homicide.
- A civil claim for damage to property.
- A civil claim for personal injury.

LOOTING

By-standers may appear helpful but be aware of what they seek to get out of it; both overtly and covertly.

The best thing to do is try and AVOID at all costs – use local information and social media to stay informed. If you become caught up in public disorder suddenly and unexpectedly, the following may help:

- Always be familiar with your surroundings so you know where your escape routes are should you encounter a mob.

- Carry small amounts of cash with you in case you need to quickly arrange transportation, pay off looters, or address your basic needs.

- Remain calm. Riots bring intense emotions boiling to the surface, but if you want to survive one, you'd be better off keeping your own emotions in check. Avoid confrontation by keeping your head down and not standing out.

- **Don't get involved.** If you're caught in a riot, do not take sides, help or stand out. Move to the outside of the mob, stay close to the walls and other barriers, avoid bottlenecks.

- **Wear safe clothes.** Wear clothes that minimize the amount of exposed skin. Do not wear anything that looks like a uniform. Do not be mistaken for a rioter, avoid black clothing, especially hooded sweaters and if you're caught in a riot and are wearing the same sweatshirt as the rioters, take it off.

On Foot.

- **Walk**. If you run, you might attract unwanted attention. Remove yourself from the situation as fast as possible.

- **Keep your friends close.** Grip hands or lock elbows with all the people in your group. If you're with a child, hold him in your arms so he doesn't get trampled. Sticking together with your friends should be your priority -- your second should be finding a way out.

- Move away by going with the flow of foot traffic, not against it.

- Though you may want to run for your life, you should move calmly and not run.

- Continue to move with the crowd until you can escape into a doorway, an alley, a side street, or a safe building.

- Avoid shops as these are often looted

On Foot...Cont.

- **Move to a safe enclosed area.** Riots most commonly happen outside on the streets, not inside buildings. Just by moving inside a sturdy and controlled building, you can protect yourself from the riot.

- Lock the doors and windows and stay away from them. Though you may be tempted to watch the riot from the windows, this will increase your chances of getting hurt.

- Move to rooms that do not lead directly outside, to avoid getting hit by stones, bullets or other missiles.

- Look for at least two exits in the building in case you need to leave in a rush. Look out for fire.

- If there are no escape routes and there is a defined base line of police with safety behind, then as a last option, approach with your hands up and open and ask for their safe transit and protection.

TEAR GAS

- Avoid tear gas. It could disable you for a period and will remain as an irritant on your clothes and skin.

- If you become contaminated by tear gas, copious amounts of water to the eyes or affected area will help.

- Tear gas (or CS gas) evaporates, so an open windy location will help.

- CS gas can be delivered by police mixed with a liquid (water canon or spray). It then evaporates into gas.

- Police should carry a neutralizing agent.

In a car.

- **Drive appropriately if you're in a car.** Stay in the car and continue driving if possible.

- Remember that you're in a position of power when you're driving. Don't let a few angry people stop you from driving your car and keep going unless you absolutely can't.

- Many activists are afraid of cars because there have been cases of any drivers running down the protesters on the roads. Remember to be firm, but not aggressive, to avoid giving the wrong impression.

- If you are caught in traffic with no way of escaping, stay in the car unless it is unsafe to do so.

- If you exit the car, stay together by exiting all from the same side.

- Carry only the essential bags – 'Grab' bag and money pouch.

- Move as fast as you can away from the riot to a safe place – see actions while on foot on the previous page.

Being followed is frequently a precursor to being attacked. Situational awareness is critical. Be suspicious; build that into your psyche. Even if you are not the driver observe the following:

- Be very aware of all the traffic / people around you.

- Look for the following vehicles (especially motorbikes) or slow-moving vehicles in your vicinity if there is no apparent reason.

- Frequent use of your mirrors and awareness of what cars are always behind or near you.

- Vary your routes to confuse would be followers.

- As you approach your destination be extra vigilant and look for people around the entrance and those that might be following.

- If you think you are being followed do not go to your destination.

- Stay in well lit, busy areas where possible.

- Use junctions and turns late and don't use your indicators.

- Drive to a safe location (police station) if you think you are being followed.

Parking and approaching your car

- Scan your location as you are approaching your – even if you are not driving.

- Ensure you don't park in isolated, badly lit areas if possible.

- Park your car reverse in and preferably close to an exit.

- Scan under the car when returning to it and see if there is anything suspicious on or around your car – spills, handprints, flat tires etc.

- If you are suspicious do not commit to entering and instead walk past and away. You can then watch from a distance.

- Do not leave valuables or anything that might attract attention on display in the car.

- Lock doors immediately on entering your car.

- If the law allows, tint all windows except the windscreen. What they can't see, they won't want.

AVOID, AVOID, AVOID

See previous page on being followed to help prevent the carjacking happening.

Most carjacking's:

- Happen when you are entering a premises, at a petrol station, at a junction, at a choke point, speed bumps, dead corner for example.
- Are usually carried out by groups of 2 to 10, on foot and often on motorbikes.
- Can involve short term abduction to extricate cash and valuables.
- Can become violent.
- Happen just before midnight so that the attackers can use ATM cards twice in a short period.
- Happen very quickly, with armed criminals closing in fast from multiple directions.
- Involve firearms.

AVOID, AVOID, AVOID

- Understand the methods used in various countries – the good Samaritan, the bump method, flashing lights, number plate, eggs etc.

- Identify possible threats and keep moving.

- At junctions leave space between you and the car in front of the exit.

- Keep doors and windows always locked and up.

- Don't stop or open windows and doors unless necessary.

Your priority is to stay alive and stay calm, so you are not injured or killed. Assume that carjackers are brutal and have no respect for life. If you are carjacked:

- Do not resist and do not be aggressive.

- Make no sudden movements and tell the carjackers your intended moves.

- Speak only when spoken to – answer truthfully if the attackers can verify what you tell them.

- Always keep your hands in view.

- Maintain positive body language.

- Try and position your body sideways to the attackers to give them a smaller target area.

- Most carjackers will take what they need, drive you around followed by their own car and then dump you unharmed.

- You may be taken to an ATM to remove money – do so with no fuss. This may also catch the culprits on camera.

Avoid being caught in an ambush by gathering as much intelligence about the route you are taking prior to departure. In the event of an ambush:

As pilots are taught in an emergency – AVIATE, NAVIGATE, COMMUNICATE – in that order.

- AVIATE – remain calm and always keep in control of the vehicle if possible.

- NAVIGATE – focus on removing yourself from the situation.

- COMMUNICATE – check with all passengers on status and then inform outside of situation.

You must also:

- Establish where the fire is coming from and where it is being aimed at – it might not be at you but someone near you.
- If the vehicle is drivable then remove yourself from the situation as quickly as possible. Drive on wheel rims if you must.
- If the vehicle is not drivable then exit the car on the 'safe' side and use the vehicle as cover.
- If help is nearby, stay where you are – if it is not then look for the nearest HARD cover, move there and wait.
- Establish communications with office / police etc. and ask them to send help.
- Stabilize any injuries that you may have and then anyone around you.

Your priority is to stay alive and try to stay physically and mentally fit.

The four main reasons for Kidnap are:

- Financial.
- Revenge.
- Political.
- To cause instability.

The 4 phases of kidnap and ransom are:

- Capture.
- Transport.
- Detention.
- Release or escape.

How to help you avoid becoming a kidnap victim:

- Be aware of watchers around where you work and live – situational awareness.

- Repeated sightings of the same vehicle or person/s.

- Protect residential details.

- Be suspicious of strangers that may pay unusual attention to you.

- Avoid being alone at a time or place kidnap is likely.

If you are kidnapped, prepare for the following:

- Fear & worry.

- Mistrust.

- Boredom & Loneliness and a sense of isolation.

- Inability to sleep or relax easily.

- Cramped, confined and poor conditions.

- Poor hygiene and irregular monotonous food.

- Assault, rape and torture – implied or real.

- Sensory deprivation – blindfolded, bound, darkness.

- Unusual and / or harsh discipline.

- Temperature extremes and a lack of suitable clothing for these.

In the event that you are kidnapped:

- **Attempt to** thwart the abduction. If you can escape the initial abduction attempt by whichever means, your ordeal ends right there. However, the first few minutes of a hostage-taking situation or abduction are the most dangerous, and they become more dangerous if you resist.

  The first few minutes are often the best time to resist since there are probably people around you depending on where you are.

- **Regain your composure.** Your heart will be pounding, and you will be terrified. **Calm down.**

- **Try to ascertain why you have been abducted.** If they are holding you for ransom or to negotiate the release of prisoners, you are most likely worth far more to them alive than dead, which will give you hope.

- **Follow the rescuers' instructions carefully.** Your rescuers will be on edge, and they will most likely shoot first and ask questions later. Obey all commands they give.

- **Keep a survival attitude.** Be positive. Remember, most kidnapping victims survive (91%) - the odds are with you. That said, you should prepare yourself for long captivity. Some hostages have been held for years but they kept a positive attitude, played their cards right and were eventually freed. Take it one day at a time.

- **Put your captor at ease.** Be calm. Cooperate (within reason) with your captor. Don't make threats or become violent and don't attempt to escape unless circumstances are right.

- **Be observant.** Right from the start, you should try to observe and remember as much as possible to help you plan an escape, predict your abductor's next moves, or give information to the police to aid in a rescue or to help apprehend and convict the kidnapper. You may not be able to use your eyes - you may be blindfolded, but you can still gather information with your sense of hearing, touch and smell.

  - Observe your captor(s).
  - How many are there?
  - Are they armed? If so, with what?
  - Are they in good physical condition?
  - What do they look and/or sound like?
  - How old are they?
  - Do they seem well-prepared?
  - What are their emotional states?
  - Observe your surroundings.
  - Where are you being taken? Visualize the route the abductors take. Make note of turns, stops and variations in speed.
  - Where are you being held? Take in as much detail as possible about your surroundings.
  - Observe yourself: How are you bound or otherwise incapacitated? How much freedom of movement do you have?

- **Keep your dignity.** It is generally psychologically harder for a person to kill, rape or otherwise harm a captive if the captive remains "human" in the captor's eyes. Do not grovel, beg or become hysterical. Try not to cry. Do not challenge your abductor but show him/her that you are worthy of respect.

- **Attempt to establish a rapport with your abductor.** If you can build some sort of bond with your captor, he/she will generally be more hesitant to harm you.

- **Avoid insulting your abductor or talking about potentially sensitive subjects.**

- **Be a good listener.** Care about what your captor has to say. Don't patronize them but be empathetic and they'll feel more comfortable around you and more benevolent toward you. Being a good listener can also help you gather information that would be useful for an escape or to help police apprehend the abductor after you're freed.

- **Try to communicate with other captives.** If you are held with other captives, talk to them as much as is safely possible. If you look out for each other and have others to talk to, your captivity will be easier to handle.

- **Keep track of time and try to discern patterns.** Keeping track of time can help you establish routines that will enable you to maintain your dignity and your sanity, give you mental challenges and help post release.

- **Establish a routine.** Wake, wash, eat, exercise, read, eat etc.

- **Divide your room up like a house.** Have a sleep area, reading area, toilet, exercise area etc.

- **Stay mentally active.** Think about what you'll do when you get back home. Hold conversations in your head with friends and loved ones. Do these things consciously - you'll be keeping yourself sane. Captivity can be boring and mind-numbing.

- **Stay physically active.** It can be difficult to remain in shape in captivity, especially if you're restrained, but it's important to do so if possible. Being in good physical condition can aid in your escape and keep you in good spirits during your captivity.

- **Ask for small favors.** If you're settled in for a long captivity, gradually ask for small accommodations. Request a heavier blanket, for example, or a newspaper. Ask for medication if you need it.

- **Blend in.** If you are held with other captives, do not stand out.

- **Meditation**. If you know nothing about meditation now, try to learn. It is useful in everyday life. It is a means of controlling your mind and therefore everything the brain does consciously. It will also help control your emotions and keep you calm.

- **Watch out for warning signs.** If your captors decide to kill you, you need to know as soon as possible so that you can plan an escape.

 If they suddenly stop feeding you, if they treat you more harshly (dehumanizing you), if they suddenly seem desperate or frightened, or if other hostages are being released but your captors don't appear to intend to release you, be ready to make your best move.

If they suddenly stop hiding their identities after wearing masks etc., this is a very strong sign that they are planning to kill you, so escape as quickly as possible.

- **Try to escape only if the time is right.** If you assess that the conditions outside your place of incarceration are suitable, keep escape at the front of your mind.

When is the right time to escape? Sometimes it's safest to just wait to be freed or rescued. However, if the perfect situation presents itself - if you have a solid plan and are almost certain that you can successfully escape - you should take advantage of the opportunity.

- **Stay out of the way if a rescue attempt is made**. The rescue attempt is a dangerous time in a hostage situation. Your captors may become desperate and attempt to use you as a shield or they may simply decide to kill hostages.

  Even if your captors are taken by surprise, you could be killed by the actions of rescuers.

  When a rescue attempt occurs, try to hide from your captors, if possible. Stay low, and protect your head with your hands, or try to get behind a protective barrier (under a desk or table, for example, or in a bathtub).

  Don't make sudden movements when armed rescuers burst in and let them know who you are.

TERRORISM – Actions on

Being aware of your surroundings, expecting anything and being prepared for everything will help save your life.

Preparing for Terrorism and avoiding it:

- Check on Western Consulate security websites for any security alerts.

- Evacuate should there be an incident – do not return to the incident as there is often a secondary blast.

- Always have a rendezvous point if you are with friends and get separated.

- Identify tourist and western hangouts and shops and stay away.

- Stay away from demonstrations or large gatherings.

- Always be aware of an evacuation route wherever you are and the way back to the safe area (hotel, office).

- Have good self-awareness of everything and everyone around you.

- When sitting in a restaurant on the street be aware of where you sit. Avoid sitting near glass windows; sit with your back to the wall facing the entrance etc.

- In restaurants and offices etc., know where the escape routes are and sit near them.

- Avoid bottlenecks, corridors and dead ends.

- Remain silent in your hiding place and **put your phone on silent**.

- If you are in your hotel room, lock yourself in, barricade the door, close the curtains and find a corner protected by hard cover.

- If you see emergency service personnel, follow their instructions and always keep your hands visible or up.

- If you can escape, do so as fast as possible using your pre-planned escape route.

If there is a bomb blast:

- Move away from the area as quickly as possible – there are often secondary blasts.

- If you are injured, attend to yourself before anyone else.

- Stay calm.

- Stay with your friends and colleagues while you evacuate.

- Stay away from glass shop fronts in case of further blasts.

- Obey all orders given by the police or emergency services.

- Make your way to a safe area – hotel, hospital, office.

- Watch local news (this is often more accurate than the international stations) for any updates.

What to do after a terrorist attack:

- Stay calm as the situation can be extremely stressful and it is likely you will go into shock, particularly if you saw terrible scenes.

- Contact family, friends, colleagues and embassy and let them know you are OK.

- Write down what you saw before and after the blast as it may help authorities in any investigations you are asked to assist in.

If you are injured in a terrorist attack:

- Try your best to stabilize yourself.

- Get yourself to medical aid as quickly as possible.

- Be conscious that all medical facilities will be busy and/or over stretched with a major attack.

- Again, call friends, family, work or your Consulate to tell them of your situation and ask for help if you need it.

- Memorize your blood type and let medical staff know of any medical issues such as allergies.

- You may need your medical insurance cards.

This Field Guide serves to provide some of the basics to remind you how to travel when entering a hostile environment.

As mentioned in the summary, HEAT training is highly recommended prior to departure for the hostile environment.

May this Field Guide serve you well in your travels.

STAY ALERT

STAY AWARE

STAY SAFE

www.ingramcontent.com/pod-product-compliance
Lightning Source LLC
Chambersburg PA
CBHW050823250726
48653CB00006B/2395